Wicc

GW01085959

The Essential Wi
Guide - Wicca Magick & Spell
Casting, Wicca Beliefs, Wicca
Symbols & Witchcraft Rituals
(Wiccan Tips, Wicca Crystals,
Candles, Stones & Herbalism)

Kevin Moore © 2015

Disclaimer:

Introduction:

First off, thank you for purchasing my book "Wicca: The Essential Wicca Beginner's Guide - Wicca Magick & Spell Casting, Wicca Beliefs, Wicca Symbols & Witchcraft Rituals (Wiccan Tips, Wicca Crystals, Candles, Stones & Herbalism)". By purchasing this book you've shown you're serious about learning more on the Wiccan lifestyle. This book is intended for people new to the world of Wicca. If you're a seasoned pro, maybe you'll learn a thing or two and find some new tools or resources to help you along the way.

When I first got introduced to Witchcraft by my future wife I instantly knew that I had found something important, which up until that point, had been missing from my life. I've always felt very drawn to nature. Wicca allows me to channel my devotion and energy into living in harmony and balance with the world around me.

I've been studying Wicca for the past decade and still only feel like I'm scratching the surface. I have a good teacher as my wife grew up surrounded by it. However, I realize many of you are looking for more information on Wicca, what it's about, and how to start the path towards becoming Wiccan.
In this book I'll discuss what Wicca is and what it means to be Wiccan. I'll discuss some of the rituals and spell work involved, along with some of the necessary tools, tips, and tricks needed to help you out along the way. I'm also throwing in a handy cheat sheet and resource guide to help you continue your education.

I'm excited to begin.. Let's get started!

Chapter One: A Brief Introduction to Wicca

In this chapter, you will learn:

- A Brief Introduction to Wicca
- Different Forms of Wicca

A Brief Introduction to Wicca

Often referred to as the "Old Religion" or "Pagan Witchcraft", Wicca comes with it own set of tenets, practices, and beliefs that are rooted in ancient pagan traditions. As with other religions, there are numerous types and paths of Wicca which people can practice. Becoming a Wiccan can be a long process that demands concentration, focus, and studying. However, it can be a very satisfying and gratifying belief system to stick to and follow.

Wicca first gained attention in the early parts of the 20th century. Many attribute Gerald Gardner for bringing it to the public forefront. Wicca gradually started gaining more followers over the next few decades. It exploded in popularity when followers started insisting on having their faith recognized during the late 1950's and early 1960's. From that point, Wicca began to spread throughout Europe and across the United States, where it gained popularity among the counter culture youth of the 1960's. Over the years it has continued to gain in popularity and new forms of Wicca have increasingly popped up all over the world.

Wicca is primarily based on believing that there is a Goddess that is at the center of all creation and life. Depending on which version of Wicca you practice, some weigh gods and goddesses equally, believing there to be balance and duality in the world. While duotheism is often seen as traditional Wicca, there are other Wiccan beliefs that range from polytheism to monism to pantheism.

In Wicca there aren't any holy books, saints, prophets, or other forms of intermediaries. Anyone practicing Wicca is said to have direct access to the Divine or Goddess. The Divine is said to live in each and every person.

The Wiccan Creed or Rede, is a central tenet followed by Wiccans that states: "If You Harm None, Do What You Will". Wicca values the harmony we should live our life by. Wiccans believe that as long as we aren't harming others, or infringing on their way of life, we should be able to proceed as we see fit. Another big belief among Wiccans is the the threefold rule. This basically means whatever actions you take will end up coming back to you threefold. The threefold rule applies to both negative and positive actions.

In Wicca, a person takes responsibility for any actions they take. Wiccans believe that a person has to be responsible for their actions and words. It's completely on the individual how they react to any outside forces or issues. Wiccans believe that accepting responsibility and making amends are the best way to handle things when you've made a mistake.

The concept of harmony with nature is an important aspect to the Wiccan lifestyle. Wiccans believe that all life is sacred. People are living in a partnership with the earth, and are reliant on the bounty the world provides in order to survive. Wiccans believe that life and nature occur in one big cycle and that we as humans are a part of this cycle.

This also leads to the belief in some form of reincarnation depending on the type of Wicca you practice. It is not a central practice so not all forms believe in it. For those that do, it stems from the fact that things in nature always keep returning. For example sea water evaporates and becomes clouds, clouds eventually give us rain. Death like life is just another part of nature's cycle.

Different Forms of Wicca

Over the years, Wicca has continued to evolve, leading to the many different forms that are being practiced today. In this next section, I'm going to discuss a few of the main forms of Wicca being practiced, some of there rituals, along with some of there beliefs. There are many other forms of Wicca being practiced. This is just a little more information for you on a few of the larger, more popular forms.

Gardnerian

This form of Wicca was founded by a man named Gerald B Gardner. He is one of the most important figures in Wicca, as he is primarily referred to as the father of modern Wicca. The reason for this is he was the first to come out in public about his beliefs. Gardnerian Wicca requires a person be initiated. This form of Wicca works within a strict degree system. Much of the information taught in this form must be held secret under oath, therefore cannot be shared with people outside their path. Some believe this form to be the only true form of Wicca, but that is a hotly debated argument.

In this system, the idea of Goddess over God is emphasized a great deal. Gardnerian Wicca follows a more structured religion, one that has a well defined hierarchy within each of their groups or covens. However, different covens have little or no authority over each other. In each each coven there exists a matriarchy, with a High Priestess normally considered the one in charge. This is not always the case, there are exceptions.

The Gardnerian practitioners view the Goddess as having three faces. Those faces are comprised of the maiden, the mother, and the crone. There is also a male consort that is referred to by a variety of different names.

The Gardnerian practitioners hold many ceremonies and celebrations throughout the year, either celebrating the different holidays based on the Wheel of the Year calendar, or to initiate members into a higher level.

Alexandrian

This form of Wicca was originally founded by a man named Alex Sanders. This form of Wicca is very influenced by the Gardnerian form of Wicca. They both use initiations and degree systems. The main difference between the two is that Alexandrian Wicca put a heavy focus on a sense of equality between both the God and Goddess. They also focus heavily on performing ceremonial magik during Sabbats and Esbats.

Traditionalist

This is a form of Wicca that is normally used to describe the first of the Wiccan traditions, predating all other forms that are practiced today. It started with the British, and members can be initiated only by someone who is a member.

Traditionalist Wiccans must continue to maintain a high level of practices and training. They believe in structure. Each of these groups are based on the myths, literature, traditions, and folktales of their demographic and geographic region. Their beliefs are mix between Gardnerian and Alexandrian Wicca.

Seax

This form of Wicca was found originally by a man named Raymond Buckland. This form of Wicca is also sometimes referred to as Saxon Wicca. While this is a traditional form of Wicca, the main difference between this and some of the aforementioned forms is that Seax Wicca has public open rituals. Following this path also doesn't require any type of initiation into a lineage. Seax Wiccans are allowed to either practice in covens or on their own. They realize that not all areas will have a coven nearby to practice with, therefore members are allowed to self initiate and practice alone. These people are often called Solitaires.

Seax Wicca also encourages its Priests and Priestesses to modify or add practices and rituals as they deem is necessary when no regulations are already in place. In Seax Wicca you normally deal with Germanic Runes and Deities for any type of divination.

Celtic

This form of Wicca combines Gardnerian and Druid Wicca. Celtic Wicca places a big emphasis on nature, the elements, and the Ancient Ones. Celtic Wicca believe in the magik and healing properties of stones, plants, trees, flowers, elemental spirits, faeries, and gnomes.

Overall this form of Wicca uses the same general theology, beliefs, and rituals that are employed by other paths of Wicca. The main difference is they use their own Celtic figures, deities, and seasonal holidays.

Eclectic

This form of Wicca combines many different traditions to form new traditions. Eclectic Wicca can be either practiced alone or in covens. People who follow this form of Wicca don't follow any one denomination, magickal practice, sect, or set of traditions. Instead, they are constantly learning and studying from a variety of different paths, applying what they think works best.

Blue Star Witchcraft

This form denounces the term Wicca and only refers to Witchcraft or Witches. This form of witchcraft uses many of the same beliefs and rituals as Gardnerian Wicca. They both use a degree system and initiations, however, in Blue Star Witchcraft they use a 5 level system instead of a 3 degree one.

Dianic

This form of Wicca was born out of Feminism. It focuses almost entirely on the Goddess and anything feminine. It allows for either female covens, mixed covens or individual practitioners. This form of Wicca honors Sabbats but doesn't have a ton of continuity in its rituals. Dianic Wicca also encourages females be in leadership roles and insists on having a Priestess in attendance to open a circle.

Chapter Two: The World of Wicca

In this chapter, you will learn:

- Gods & Goddesses
- Wiccan Belief Systems
- The Wiccan Calendar

Gods & Goddesses

Wicca mainly revolves around worship of a goddess and a god. However, what two deities these are represented by often vary by group or individual practitioner. While most religions from the West are monotheistic (one god), Wiccans can believe in many different variations depending on the form of Wicca they practice and what deities call to them. This can make it difficult for people to understand Wiccans and their faith. Most people are used to following and believing in a singular being.

Primarily, Wiccans are united by practice, instead of by belief. Many Wiccans find themselves called to by different deities. Wicca has no one pantheon. Some may honor Apollo, while others may honor Freya or Mars. Just because I don't happen to follow the same gods as one of my fellow Wiccans doesn't mean I think they are wrong for doing so. It just means that those particular gods don't call out to me.

Many of those who consider themselves to be traditionalists will follow whoever their covens gods are. Eclectics on the other hand, will often have their own personal practices, saying it was their gods who reached out to them.

Many Wiccans such as traditionalists take oaths of secrecy, which won't allow them to publicly name their gods. That's why in many texts Gods and Goddess where used to describe their deities instead.

There are thousands of different gods a Wiccan may worship. Each culture has it own set of Gods and Goddesses that may call out to a practitioner. There are no wrong and right answers when it comes to who you believe in.

The Horned God and the Triple Goddess

These were terms that were used by the early writers of Wicca. They were meant more as descriptions of their gods, and were not meant to act as their actual names. However, over the years many Wiccans have adopted them both as names.

The Horned God is used to represent the male part of certain Wiccans belief systems. He is commonly associated with wilderness, nature, hunting, sex, and life. When he is depicted, he's shown as having antlers or horns on his head. He is also shown having the head of beast on a human body. This is to help emphasize the union of animal (including humanity) and the divine.

The Triple Goddess or Moon Goddess is used to represent the female part of certain Wiccans belief systems. She is frequently depicted as the maiden, the mother, and the crone.

The Maiden represents inception, enchantment, youth, birth, new beginnings, and the waxing moon.

The Mother represents fertility, ripeness, stability, sexuality, life, and the full moon.

The Crone represents endings, wisdom, death, and the waning moon.

Nature Spirits

When I think of nature spirits I think of more local entities that live within a particular rock, tree, or river. Not all Wiccans believe in nature spirits. For those people that do believe, they will often interact with them or show them respect. This does not mean they worship them. It just means they respect them.

Elementals

These are non corporeal entities that are composed of one element entirely. Those elements include Air, Fire, Water and Earth. Unlike gods, we often command an elemental to accomplish a task instead of worshiping them.

Spirit

Often referred to as the 5th element. This is an element that is present in everything, whether it's animate or inanimate. It's known as the binding force through which all manifestation becomes possible. It's normally represented by the color white. It doesn't have any assigned gender and type of energy. It's not related to one season but instead the whole Wheel of the Year.

The Afterlife

Wiccans normally believe in some form of afterlife. It's not a place where we'll spend all eternity like Heaven or Hell, instead it's where we'll spend time before being reincarnated. It's known by many names and you may find it referenced as the Otherworld, the Summerland, the Afterlife, and the Shining Land. When divining, many Wiccans believe this is the source of the answers they are given. Many Wiccans believe this place is where we make our decisions on what our next incarnation will be, based on all the things we learned or haven't yet learned in previous lives.

Reincarnation

Many Wiccans believe that we have lived many different lives over the years. Depending on the person or the coven, many Wiccans believe they can come back as any living creature be it human, animal or plant. On the other hand some Wiccans believe you can only be reincarnated as human.

Reincarnation is celebrated often in the Wiccan belief system. Many Wiccans perform dream analysis, past life progression, and meditation techniques in order to try and recall some of there former lives. They can then use that knowledge to help them make better decisions about the future.

Wiccan Belief Systems

Wicca has no one higher authority, bible, or belief system. However, an attempt was made in the 1970's to help put forth some general principles, in order for the general public to have a better understanding of Witchcraft and help distinguish it from some of the many misconceptions it faced. For example, that Wicca was the same as Satanism.

What came out of those attempts was 13 different principles of Wiccan belief. Here I'll outline each of those beliefs as they are still endorsed by many Wiccans today. Remember, since there is no one belief system, not all of these may hold true for every form of Wicca being practiced. It's meant to give a better overall understanding of Wicca in general.

1. Wiccans practice rites to help attune themselves with life forces marked by the Seasonal Cross Quarters and Quarters, along with the different phases of the moon.

2. Wiccans realize their intelligence imbues them with a responsibility toward protecting the environment. Living in harmony with all nature around us is the goal.

3. Wiccans realize that there is a power that is far greater than what the normal person believes in. It is often referred to as supernatural, however Wiccans view it as potential to all.

4. Wiccans believe in a both inner and outer worlds. Known as the collective unconsciousness and spiritual world. Wiccans neglect neither of these dimensions, realizing that both are necessary in order to achieve fulfillment.

5. Wiccans believe in a creative power that lies in all people, and values masculinity and feminine as equal with neither above the other, both supporting one another. Sex is a symbol and also an embodiment of life. It is also a source of energy that is used in worship and magickal practice.

6. Wiccans don't recognize authoritarian hierarchies, instead they honor anyone that teaches, and they respect people that share their wisdom and knowledge.

7. Wiccans see magick, wisdom, and religion as all being united in the way a person sees the world and lives their lives within it. Witchcraft is a life philosophy and world view, also referred to as the Wiccan Way.

8. Wiccans only animosity towards other philosophies and religions is the way those institutions try and claim they are the only way, while trying to deny and suppress the freedom of others who believe differently and want to practice their own beliefs.

9. Wiccans believe in the fulfillment and affirmation of life. Wiccans believe in the universe around them and the role they play within that universe.

10. Wiccans aren't Wiccan simply by calling oneself Wiccan. They must live the path and seek out harmony with nature.

11. Wiccans don't believe in the idea of an absolute evil. Wiccans don't worship entities referred to as the Devil or Satan. Wiccans do not seek to gain power through other people's suffering. Wiccans don't accept that benefiting personally should be derived from someone else being denied.

12. Wiccans are not threatened by having debates on the history of Witchcraft, the legitimacy of certain traditions, and how certain terminology originated. Wiccans are more concerned with their present lives and what the future holds.

13. Wiccans feel they should always look within nature to find things that will contribute to their long term well being and health.

The Wiccan Calendar

Often referred to as the "Wheel of The Year", the Wiccan calendar is a representation of our planet's year long cycle. It got the "Wheel" moniker because when you drew out a circle and then drew eight lines that all intersected in the center, the end result looked like a wheel on a wagon.

Each of the eight points on this circle reference an event or progression as each season passes. That's why, in a sense, the "Wheel" turns. Each of these turns or points on the wheel are celebrated by Wiccans. Each of these celebrations is known as a Sabbat. A Sabbat is a solar celebration and Esbats consist of lunar celebrations. Each season changing is celebrated, as is each in-between midpoint.

When looking at the wheel, the four "spokes" are labeled as either an equinox or solstice. The other four points are either marked with a harvesting or a planting. Basically, there are four major Sabbats (High Holidays) and four minor Sabbats (Low Holidays). The major ones are the ones in-between the solstice and equinoxes. The four minor Sabbats are the two solstices and the two equinoxes.

The reason this is of importance to Wiccans is because it tells us when it's the right time to plant and when it's the right time to harvest. Wiccans celebrate each turn of the wheel because it represents the progression of our lives as well. Both the earth and its people go through changes each season. The "Wheel" is also responsible for telling us the story of the Goddess and the God, along with their life cycle.

None of these holidays were invented by man. They aren't like holidays in the same way that Christmas or 4th of July is a holiday. Sabbats do not celebrate historical events. They are as old as Earth itself, even before the time of man.

Here is a little more information on the eight Sabbats, when they fall on the Wiccan calendar, and why they are important.

Yule - 12/20 – 12/22 (Changes each year.)

Yule is considered the first Sabbat on the Wiccan Calendar. It's often referred to as Winter Solstice. Yule is the longest night of the entire year. From each day until Summer Solstice the day gets longer and longer by a few minutes. The main reason Wiccans celebrate Yule is because it is the God's rebirth from Goddess. Our sun is the symbol for God, and as God grows the day grows longer. Yule also happens to represent a midpoint in the colder season. It's considered a time of rest from the harvest season, just like the Goddess rests after giving birth.

Imbolc - 02/02

Located between the winter solstice and spring equinox. This is most widely known as Groundhogs Day. It's considered when the first new signs of life begin to show after the colder months. This is also the time of year when preparations are made for the first new plantings of harvest. In the cycle of the God and the Goddess, the God is still a child but growing quickly, and the Goddess has reappeared after her rest in the form of a younger maiden.

Ostara - 3/20 – 3/22 (Changes each year)

This is known as the spring equinox. At this point of the year night and day are of equal hours and warmer weather is on the horizon. The ground is prepared for seeds as this is the first of the planting Sabbats or fertility Sabbats. In the cycle of the God and the Goddess, they are both younger adults and have begun a courtship. Just as seeds begin to come to life, so does the Goddesses womb.

Beltane – 05/01

This is considered the day when God and Goddess unite. Crops have all been planted and the Goddess is beginning to show. People often dance and gather round the maypole to celebrate the union of the God and Goddess. The maypole staff represents god, the flowers opening represent the goddesses sexual peak and pregnancy.

Litha 06/20 – 06/22 (Changes each year)

This is commonly referred to as summer solstice. It's the longest day of each calendar year. After this, nights grow longer each day until winter solstice. In the cycle of the God and Goddess, this is when God is at his peak and full strength. On the other side, the Goddess is growing larger with her pregnancy as crops also continue growing.

Lammas – 08/01

This is known as the celebration of first harvest. Many new crops have begun to grow and are now ready to be harvested. In the cycle of the God and Goddess, the God begins getting weaker as the Goddess's child gets more developed in the womb. The Goddess also begins mourning the impending loss of the God but takes some comfort in the knowledge that he will be reborn in the near future.

Mabon – 09/20 – 09/22 (Changes each year)

This is referred to as the fall equinox. It is also known as the celebration of the second harvest, and also is referred to as Wiccan Thanksgiving. Night and day once again share an equal amount of hours in the day. The next round of crops are also ready for harvesting. This is also considered to be the time when we celebrate all of the bounties we received, feasting with both our friends and our community. In the cycle of the God and Goddess, this is when the God rests in preparation for his death.

Samhain - 10/31

This is referred to as Wiccan New Years Eve. It's the night where the previous year dies out and the new one begins. It is also the final celebration of harvest for the year. It is when we gather the last of our crops and prepare for the oncoming winter. In the cycle of the God and Goddess, the God has died and the Goddess begins to make the world cold as she mourns her loss. During this time the veil that is between both the living world and the world of the dead is at the thinnest point it will reach all year. Wiccans often use this time in order to try and communicate with those they love that have passed away.

** One thing to make note of is that the "Wheel of The Year" was originally from the Northern Hemisphere. Due to this fact most Wiccans advance dates six months in advance for the Southern Hemisphere, this way they line up with the seasons in those regions. **

Here is what the date changes might look like in the Southern Hemisphere:

Samhain – 04/30 or 05/01

Yule – 06/20 – 06/23 (Changes each year)

Imbolc – 07/31 or 08/01

Ostara – 09/20 – 09/23 (Changes each year)

Beltane – 10/31

Litha – 12/20 – 12/23 (Changes each year)

Lammas – 02/02

Mabon 03/20 – 03/23 (Changes each year)

Besides the Sabbats, I want to also discuss the Esbats. Here is a little more information on the Esbats, when they fall on the Wiccan calendar, and why they are important.

Esbats are generally considered to be full moon rituals, although they can technically be held at other times as well. Full moons occur 12 to 13 times a year. Many Wiccans prefer working under a full moon, but you can practice magick under any type of moon. Different kinds of energy come with differing moons. This means some moons are better for some particular forms of magick.

The different Moon cycles are:

The New Moon – This type of moon is preferred for magick that deals with new beginnings. For example, starting a new job, finding new love, or becoming a new you.

The Waxing Moon – This type of moon is preferred for magick that deals with growth. For example, growing wealth, developing love, or building on a career.

The Full Moon – This type of moon is preferred for magick that deals with really going after the things you want out of life. For example, attaining love, achieving dreams, and divining the future.

The Waning Moon – This type of moon is preferred for magick that deals with banishing things. For example, losing some weight, beating an addiction, or overcoming an illness.

The Monthly Esbats

January – Known as either the Wolf Moon, Winter Moon, Snow Moon, or Cold Moon. This is a period of strength and protection. This moon can be a time of endings and new beginnings.

February – Known as either the Storm Moon, Quickening Moon, or Death Moon. This is a period of strength and fertility.

March – Known as either the Chaste Moon, or the Worm Moon. This is a period of newness and purity, a time to begin thoughts of hope and new successes.

April – Known as either the Seed Moon, Grass Moon, Wind Moon, or Egg Moon. This is a period of sowing the seeds of magick. It's a time of planning ahead for the future.

May – Known as either the Hare Moon, Flower Moon, or the Planting Moon. This is a period of love, health, wisdom, and romance. It's a perfect time to rekindle passion and reignite old sparks.

June – Known as either the Lovers Moon, Rose Moon, or Strawberry Moon. This is a period of success, marriage, and love energy.

July – Known as either the Mead Moon, Lightning Moon, Thunder Moon, or Blessing Moon. This is a period of rebirth, strength, enchantment, success, and health. This is also a time for magick and celebration. It's a great time to practice prosperity magick.

August – Known as either the Corn Moon, Wort Moon, Red Moon, or Barley Moon. This is a period of agriculture, abundance, and marriage.

September – Known as either the Harvest Moon, or Hunters Moon. This is a period of prosperity, protection, and abundance.

October – Known as either the Blood Moon, or Falling Leaf Moon. This is a period of resolution, new goals, spirituality, and protection. This is wonderful time for divination. It's a good time to take a moment and reflect on your year , while taking account of any accomplishments.

November - Known as either the Mourning Moon, Tree Moon, or Beaver Moon. This is a period of prosperity, friendship, family, and abundance. This is another great time of year for divining what will come in the upcoming year.

December – Known as either the Oak Moon, or the Long Night Moon. This is a period of healing and hope. During this period the moon has full reign over the earth as night outweighs the day. This is the perfect time to let go of old things and start over. Banish the negative and embrace new beginnings.

Chapter Three: How to Become A Wiccan

In this chapter, you will learn:

- How to Become a Wiccan

How to Become a Wiccan

In this chapter I'm going to discuss the steps you should begin taking in order to become a practicing Wiccan. It's important to pay proper attention to each step in order to properly understand what you're doing and the reasons behind why you're doing it. I've broken the entire process down into 14 smaller segments, each of which I'll discuss in further detail down below.

1. Learn About Wicca and Wiccan Belief Systems.

I've discussed a lot about these things in the first two chapters but you should make it a point to really research what it means to be Wiccan and what you'll be expected to do once you begun practicing it yourself. You'll also want to decide what kind of Wiccan belief system fits your personal set of beliefs. Everyone is different. There's no wrong answers. You should practice the form of Wicca that works for you and your lifestyle.

On the flip side, you'll also need to learn the things that Wicca isn't. Many people often have misconceptions about what Wicca is and what it means to be Wiccan. It's just as important to know what Wicca is about, as it is to know what Wicca isn't about. Remember, Wiccans come from all walks of life. There's no one type of behavior that defines every Wiccan.

I personally devoured as many books and articles on the subject as I could find. I also networked and learned from those around me. I found it to be immensely helpful in getting me through the process.

2. Learn About Wiccan Rituals and Ceremonies.

Study! Study! Study! You need to know what these are, how to perform them, and when they occur. Most Wiccans prefer to perform ceremonies and rituals outdoors close to nature unless safety or weather become an issue. Many of the ceremonies and rituals revolve around the changing of seasons and moon cycles.

Many rituals include a gathering of Wiccans in a circle surrounded by candles. This circle is said to create a space for divination, healing, nature based activities, or discussion. Quite a few rituals and ceremonies require you eat food and drink juice or wine before the ritual ends and the circle gets dissolved.

3. Learn The Ethics Behind Being Wiccan.

Many people overlook this one but it's important. This religion isn't about casting damaging spells that are meant to curse or harm others. As a Wiccan you are responsible for your use and relationship to magic. You must live by the Wiccan Rede: "If You Harm None, Do What You Will". Living in harmony with the earth and those around you, while remaining positive will make you a successful Wiccan

4. Choose Your Deities and Belief Systems.

After you've learned what being a Wiccan means and represents it's time to begin deciding what type of Wiccan you'll be and what deities and belief systems you'll follow. Wicca has followers that believe in many different gods and goddesses. There are hundreds of different deities to choose. These gods and goddesses are part of nature and don't posses superhuman abilities or powers.

It's important to learn about the different deities because one will become your patron or matron deity. For many people, their deity is revealed to them during the learning process, so be as open as you can when gathering information on the different deities. Be sure to do your homework so you know what deities have characteristics that are or aren't to your personal liking.

5. Learn The Threefold Rule.

For Wiccans, the threefold rule is that whatever you do, it will come back to you three times over. This works both for positive and negative things. Following and practicing this idea will help you become more aware of your actions, along with what the consequences are for being vindictive or vengeful.

6. Start A Journal.

As you're working your way through this process you want to take notes and observations about yourself so you can understand what is important to you as a Wiccan and what things aren't. This journal will one day become part of your personal Book of Shadows.

7. Learn About Magick.

As a Wiccan you need to learn about magick, what it is, and how to go about using it. Magick for Wiccans is the practice of gathering and channeling energy with a specific purpose in mind. The reason there is a "k" at the end of the word is to distinguish itself from the stage tricks the word is often associated with.

Many Wiccans believe magick to be a manifestation of energy that is drawn from within. It's more spiritual than sorcery. You will have to learn how to practice magick safely and what consequences casting certain spells can have.

I find that practicing visualization and meditation help to give the proper concentration needed to use magick more effectively.

8. Network With Other Wiccans.

It's important to network and connect with other people practicing Wicca. Some places you can find other Wiccans is online in forums and discussion groups. If you're lucky, you might have a thriving local community. It's easier to find like minded people in higher populated areas but I have plenty of friends who live in smaller communities and were still able to find a good amount of people who practice.

It's a good idea to discuss with other Wiccans their beliefs, how they got started, and how they go about practicing their craft. Having conversations like these will give you a deeper understanding of the Wiccan faith, what things you might want to use in practicing your own faith, and developing a community that is supportive.

9. Have A Self Dedication Ceremony.

It's important to formalize your own relationship with Wicca, while also sharing your devotion with the deities you've chosen. There are a variety of ceremonies you can choose to hold. I would suggest doing some further research online and finding a ceremony that feels right to you.

10. Join A Coven

Most formal gatherings and covens have a rule that you must have studied Wicca for at least a year before you can be deemed serious or knowledgeable enough to become a part of their group. Learn if your area has a coven. Some covens are open to new members while others are closed membership. If it's open to new members, begin introducing yourself well in advance to build relationships and let the members know you're serious about one day becoming a member.

Remember, you don't have to join a coven. Many Wiccans practice their faith alone. This is a personal preference and one that is purely up to how you want to do things.

11. Take a Oath of Secrecy.

You should take an oath of secrecy. This oath covers protection of identity, protection of any mysteries in the craft, and protection of the rituals practiced. Do not out other Wiccans. Many people are private about their faith and don't want others knowing their business. People still remain secretive due to all the negative connotations associated with Witchcraft.

Wiccans need to keep rituals a secret to maintain trust within their coven and to allow people to be vulnerable and open within the group. Respecting all the mysteries of Wicca helps to keep the practice going and reserves its magick for only those who are actively practicing.

12. Spend Time Each Day In Practice and Devotion.

Once you've completed all the steps to become Wiccan it's important to make your beliefs a part of your everyday life. Many Wiccan practices take only a few minutes a day. Some of these exercises include giving thanks, meditating and centering yourself, rituals of devotion to your deity, speaking to your deities about your problems, going out into nature, and exploring your beliefs through writing and art.

13. Celebrate the Wiccan Sabbats.

I went over Sabbats in the Wiccan Calendar section. It's important to celebrate and acknowledge these High Holidays and Low Holidays. You want to show your faith and devotion to your deities and the nature.

14. Create Your Book of Shadows

Having your own Book of Shadows is a crucial part of Wicca. This is where you record your Wiccan practice. When developing your book you can go a bunch of different routes, therefore no two Book of Shadows will be the same. These tomes are extremely personal and should be tailored to your own personal experiences. Most times, a Book of Shadows will contain a page devoted to the Wiccan Rede discussed earlier, a list of the deities that you're following, a list and description of rituals, spells, incantations, mythology and other miscellaneous things.

Chapter Four: Wicca Symbols, Tools & Terminology

In this chapter, you will learn:

- A Guide to Common Wicca Tools
- A Guide to Common Wicca Symbols & Terminology

A Guide to Common Wicca Tools

As in many other religions, tools are used to enhance and aid in rituals and worship. The tools themselves have no actual power, although they do hold powerful significance symbolically.

While using tools isn't an absolute must when practicing Witchcraft, they are good to have, even if only to help you focus your concentration and will. The most basic tools a Wiccan can start with would be elemental tools. What are those, you ask? Well, these are tools that represent one of the four life elements. For example: The Wand is for Air, The Pentacle is for Earth, The Chalice is for Water, and The Athame is for Fire.

You don't need to go out and buy a lot of these tools, or spend large amounts if you do get them. Many ordinary things around your house can become implements and substituted in as tools. If you choose, you can even make the tools yourself. Many believe that making the tools by hand means they become infused with some of your own personal power, thereby making it more effective.

However you come upon your tools you should always cleanse them of any negative energy and prior influence before using them. In order to do this, you'll want to physically clean the item and then bury it in the ground at least a few days so that any negative energy can be purified and dispersed back into the earth.

Another cleansing method is to immerse your tool in natural water, such as a river, lake or sea. Leave the item in the water for a few hours before taking the tool out and drying it off. Don't use this method if water will ruin the item. Always use common sense when cleansing your tools. Once you're tools have all been cleansed you'll want to consecrate each one so that it's ready to be used for any magickal purposes.

Below I will go over a bunch of the different tools commonly used by Wiccans, along with why they're significant. This is by no means a complete list of tools. Just some of the main ones Wiccans should be aware of.

Pentacle

This is normally made from wood, stone, or copper and comes in the form of round shaped solid disc. The disc itself will normally have an engraving of a five point star that is upright, enclosed in a circle referred to as a Pentagram. When a disc is decorated in this particular fashion it becomes know as a Pentacle.

Many traditions will add other spirits, elements, or deities as a source of additional power. A Pentacle is usually the centerpiece of a Wiccans alter and is usually what other items are placed on in order to be charged or consecrated. This tool represents Earth, and can be used at times to summon the Goddesses and Gods.

Athame

This is a Wiccans ritual traditional dagger. Normally it is a double edged blade made of steel with a black colored handle. Most Wiccans will engrave the blade or handle with magickal symbols of elements, spirits, or deities to give it another source of power. This item is a command tool, it's used direct the power that passes through it. The Athame is often used to cast circles, consecrate items, charge objects, and cast away negative energy.

Most Wiccans do not use there Athame as a regular knife. It is used only for magickal purposes. In most traditions this elemental tool is associated with Fire, although in some it's connected to Air.

Chalice

This often represents the Water element. It's seen as symbolizing containment and is often used to help represent the Goddess and her womb. The base of the Chalice is symbolic of our material world around us. The stem of the Chalice is representative of our connection between the spirit and man. The opening or rim of the Chalice is used to symbolize the receiving of spiritual energy.

The chalice will normally be made of material from olden times. Shells, gourds and horns were often used for holding sacred fluids during a ritual, and then eventually silver became the preference of most Wiccans as it's associated with the Goddess and the moon. The Chalice is used during rituals to hold blessed wine and water. Traditionally, many covens pass around the Chalice to all members so they can take a sip in a show of unity.

Wand

This is considered to be one of the main magickal tools of any Wiccan. Normally the Wand is crafted from a tree that is considered sacred. Some sacred trees are Elder, Willow, Oak, Peach, Apple, Cherry and Hazel. The Wand should be about a foot in length and nowadays is often tipped with gems and crystals.

The Wand is used as an invocation tool, used to help evoke the spirits, Gods and Goddesses. The Wand is also used when bestowing blessings, charging objects, and drawing down the moon while during a ritual. For most Wiccan traditions this tools represents the Air element, although in a few it can represent the Fire element.

Broom

This is a ritual tool most Wiccans use as it is sacred to both God and Goddess. Traditionally, this tool is made of three separate woods. Birch twigs are used for the brush, Ash is used on the handle, and Willow is used to make the cord that binds it together. Birch is used because it purifies and draws a spirit into a person's service. Ash is used because it has command over all four elements and is protective. Willow is used because it is something that is sacred in the eyes of the Goddess.

The Broom has many purposes in Wicca, but it's main purpose is to protect and purify. This tool is used to cleanse areas before any magick is practiced by sweeping any astral or negative energy away. Some Wiccans would also place this item under their pillows or beds for protection. Some Wiccans hung it over their doorways so evil couldn't enter.

Censer

This tool is used for containing any burning incense used during a ritual. It doesn't matter what type of censer a Wiccan uses. For instance, I've always just used a bowl that was filled up with sand as mine. This tool represents the Air element, and will usually be placed before images of the God and Goddess on an altar.

Book of Shadows

This tool is essentially a Wiccans workbook. Within its pages, rituals, invocations, guidelines, runes, spells, rules, poems, symbols, and chants are all recorded. This Book of Shadows is normally always written by the hand of the individual who owns it. Many covens will have newer initiates copy their teacher's book exactly by hand, then adding their own material as they continued to progress. In today's society, people often use technology and computerize their Book of Shadows.
I prefer the old Tradition of having a handwritten book. I think using a loose leaf book is best. This allows you to shuffle pages around when getting ready for a ritual. However, this is just my personal preference feel free to use whatever method you want when creating your own Book of Shadows.

Cauldron

Besides the broom, this is probably the item most connected to Witchcraft. The Cauldron is a container where germination, transmutation, and transformation can occur. This tool is symbolic of the Goddesses womb, and is the manifestation of fertility and femininity. All things are born out of the Goddesses Cauldron, and eventually all things return to it. This item is also a symbol of the Water element, and is often associated with inspiration, immortality, and reincarnation.

The practical purpose of the Cauldron is for making potions, brews, and containing smaller fires that will be used with spells. This item can also be used for divination or scrying, by filling it up with water and then gazing into it.

Traditionally, this tool is made out of cast iron and sits on three legs. A Cauldron normally has an opening that is smaller then the widest part. These items can come in any size and are a cherished possession of most Wiccans.

Bolline

This is the practical knife used by Wiccans. In the past this was used for harvesting herbs and the blade was a sickle shape. Today, this is normally just a regular knife that can be used for carving and cutting. Bolline normally have a white handle so you can easily differentiate it from the black handle of the Athame.

This knife is used during any ritual function that requires a knife be used for mundane tasks like cutting flowers, cutting cords and carving symbols into candles.

Candles

A Wiccan ceremony isn't complete with candles. Many believe the candle represent either God or the Goddess. Some use it to indicate the Fire element. Candles are used in rituals to help symbolize concepts, people and emotions. Candles are also used heavily in spell casting, with different color candles having different uses.

Crystals

These are powerful tools as they emanate and hold healing energy. Many Wiccans use crystals in spell casting, some carry them to absorb healing energy, while others place them around their homes. Crystal quartz is often considered to be the most versatile crystal. It's a powerful energy amplifier and can hold the charge of any vibration. Other crystals have more specific uses. For instance, citrine is used for abundance, rose quartz is used for love, and onyx is used for protection.

Altar

This is a main component to any Wiccans tool set. In an ideal situation you'll have a room that is designated specifically for your altar. These can be as simple or as elaborate as you'd like to make them.

The altar serves two purposes. First, it's an ideal spot to keep your other materials and tools. Second, it's the visual focus of your ritual magick work. Depending on the traditions you follow, you may want to have your altar facing in a specific direction. Place it wherever you think it should go. You want to be able to view it easily, where you'll also be able to have access to it and any other tools you'll be using.

The left side of an altar is normally reserved for the Goddess and the right side is reserved for the God. Tools sacred to each are placed on their respective sides. This means on the left side you'll place tools like the Chalice, Pentacle, Cauldron, and Bell. On the right side you'll place tools like the Wand, Censor, Bolline, and Athame. Also on the right side you'll normally place a gold, yellow or red candle to represent the God. On the left side you'll put a silver, green, or white candle.

Bell

This is tool used in rituals for banishment and invocation. This is a feminine symbol of the Goddess and her creative force. This tool is often used to indicate the start of ritual by banishing any negative energy before beginning. It is also used in rituals to invoke the Goddess, and can be sounded to call forth Elementals and Watchers.

The Bell is also used to guard homes and ward off evil spirits or spells. They are normally hung on doors or placed inside a cupboard. When hung from some type of cord, a Bell comes to symbolize the soul of humanity suspended between earth and heaven.

Sword

This is another command tool. It's not often used, but may be necessary during some spells. The size, length, and style of the Sword are all personal preferences, just be sure you're able to easily wield the Sword you choose. This is also a Fire element.

Robes

This tool is the final thing I'll go over in this tools section. Robes are important as they can often be a fundamental piece of magickal gear. Robes can be either decorated or plain, and they can be any color you desire as long as that color gives you a more magickal feel.

Many Wiccans have more than one color robe and match them to the color of the candles used in the spells their working on. The idea of the Robes is to feel more at ease. The robes don't need to be fashionable, and of course if you don't want to wear one you can wear something that works for you.

A Guide to Common Wicca Symbols & Terminology

So what is a Wiccan Symbol? Well, in simple terms, it's anything representing Wicca. There are four common categories that Wiccan symbols fall into. Those are items used when practicing Wicca, things that are linked historically to Wicca, symbols for the Gods and Goddesses, and symbols that have been adopted by Wiccans over the years,.

In this section I'll discuss some of the common symbols you'll run across and what they mean. This is by no means a complete list. I'm just pointing out some of the ones I think you should know starting out. You'll learn of many more during your future studies.

Ankh

Also known as the "Cross of Life". This has been adopted as a Wiccan symbol over the years but is originally based in Egyptian lore. The Ankh is a union of the God and Goddess symbols. Those being the oval of the female Goddess and the staff or cross of the God. It is meant to symbolize the universe's creative power.

Aura

This is the field of energy that surrounds things, especially living things. Everything either living or not living has an aura, as everything is made from energy. Many people perceive an aura as either light or color. Wiccans develop their abilities to try and sense these fields of energy.

Bat

These have become Wiccan symbols for a few reasons. Some of theses reasons are because of their night time affinity. Another is because they use different senses then most to maneuver. Also, they are thought to have shamanic power in many circles.

Bonfire

Things like bonfires represent the Fire element. Fire is considered to be the main transformative force in nature, and represents Divine Light. Fire is normally invoked at most, if not every, Wiccan celebration. It's said when you jump through a Bonfire you are momentarily passing through a purifying flame. That means once you've passed through it you'll come out on the other end cleansed.

Most Wiccans will often jump through the fire two times. The first time is to purge away the old, while the second time is to empower all the new. Prior to jumping the first time, you declare or think of what you want to release from your life. Prior to jumping the second time, you set yourself an intention of what you want to bring into your life.

Cats

These creatures are often thought to perceive things that are beyond our own physical world. Cats are thought to be sensitive to many different types of energy and are seen as making a great companion to a Wiccan working magick. Many Wiccans believe that cats can protect a Wiccan while their working, while also acting as messenger to the spirit realm. This makes them ideal familiars.

Circle

This is a prominent Wicca symbol. The Spiral of Life, Circle of Earth and Wheel of the Year are all based off the circle and the importance of nature's cyclical existence. This is why Wiccans often gather in Circles when doing spells, celebrations, and rituals.

Cloak

They have a symbolic function in Wicca. They are like Robes in that they cover us without being restrictive. This allows open space so that the Divine can enter. They also are great from a practical viewpoint as they can hide pockets carrying all your tools and implements.

Crone

This is a stage of life in women and one aspect of the concept known as Triple Goddess. The Crone is normally considered to be the Goddess of Wisdom. That's because she no longer sheds her wise lunar blood but instead keeps it within her body.

Wiccans to this day still venerate the Crone. They have a perception of power bestowed upon them by years of knowledge and experience. Many Wiccans will actually celebrate when they go through Croning themselves, holding a ritual of passage once they've reached the end of menopause.

Divination

Most Wiccans perform some type of divination. These can include Scrying, Tea Leaves, Dowsing, Tarot Cards, and Palm Reading. In reality Wiccans are constantly reading messages that are sent from the Divine. These messages come in sudden ideas, life events, feelings, and coincidences.

Dogs

Dogs, especially black ones, are heavily identified with Wiccans as their Familiars.

Dowsing

This is when Wiccans search for things that are hidden by using a crystal, stick, or some other form of tool. Dowsing is commonly used to find water, minerals, oils or anything else a Wiccan might need or be drawn to. Depending on what you're dowsing for depends on what type of tool you may need to use, For example, Willow works well for dowsing for water.

Energy

Energy work is a classic Wicca symbol. The idea of raising, shifting and directing energy is what Wicca is about in many respects.

Evil Eye

This one has become more and more closely associated with Wicca and Witches over the years. The Evil Eye comes from a myth about the Goddess Maat, and how her All Seeing Eye was able to tell a person's soul by just having a glance at them. Over time this idea of telling and assessing a person's soul turned into cursing a person's soul at just a glance.

Since receiving the Evil Eye is mainly seen as being given by a woman, the cures for the Evil Eye derive from symbols that are feminine or Goddess in nature. Those symbols include Black Cats, Cowrie Shells, and Kali's Black Pot.

Familiars

This is a popular Wicca symbol. Any animal may be a Familiar to a Wiccan. Some are more helpful in terms of practicing Witchcraft. Animals closely associated as common Familiars are Cats, Bats, Black Dogs, Frogs, Snakes, Ravens, and Owls.

Feather

This is a Wicca symbol that represents the ability of flight, and our spirit's freedom to gain access into different realms. Feathers are most commonly used to represent the Air element when placed on a Wiccan Altar. One thing to note is feathers should always be purified or blessed before being used.

Frogs

In Wicca these animals are known for their ability to move freely between worlds. That's because they both live on land and water. Wiccans relate to this because they live in both the spiritual world and mundane world.

Ghost

Ghosts symbolize the time of year when those who've passed can once again revisit this world. Wiccans are known for communicating with their loved ones even after they've passed much like in many other cultures and religions.

Goddess

Many Wiccans wear the Goddess symbol as she is interwoven with most Wiccan rituals and beliefs. People worship different Goddesses. For example, the Earth Goddess, the Moon Goddess, the Triple Goddess and the Star Goddess. There are hundreds of Gods and Goddesses to choose from. Each culture has their own rich history filled with different deities.

Grove

This is a small forest known as a traditional place of worship for Wiccans. This is often compared to a Wiccan cathedral. You have the trees acting as guardians, and under the moon and stars, you feel the Divine presence around you.

Herbs

Wicca is known for its association with nature based healing. This is primarily done through the use of herbs, poultices and different teas. Herbs play an important role in Wiccan spells and are often used as both magickal and healing agents.

Incense

This is a Wiccan tool that also carries symbolic meaning. Smoke is representative of our intentions and prayers rising upwards towards the Divine. Certain scents given off by incense have the power to shift our conscious mind to the energy in plants. Incense is often seen on Wiccan altars representing the Air element.

Menstruation

This is sacred to Wiccans. The reason for this is that it is the magickal and voluntary shedding of life essence, a woman's blood, without any wounds or harm. The word itself is derived from the word "moon". It's connection to one of the world's greatest powers, a woman's ability to give birth, makes it sacred in many circles.

Midwife

Midwives have held a close association with Witchcraft for a long time. This is due to there ability to heal using both their skills and herbs. Midwives are also attendants to birth, the gateway from the realm of spirit to our physical world. They have the ability to change an outcome on whether a newborn is born healthy or dies during labor.

Mirror

This is a Wiccan ritual symbol and tool. They are believed to directly reflect a person's soul. The mirror is representative of the Divine, reflected in a form we can see in the physical world. It is said that when one looks in a Wiccan ritual mirror they have the ability to see the God or Goddess that is within them. It acknowledges the belief that everything is the Divine. This tool is often used in divination. For example some look into mirrors to try and see into the future. It's important as both a tool and as a symbol.

Moon

The Moon is considered the main Wiccan Goddess. The Moon is more than a symbol. It represents the Feminine part of the Divine. It helps to balance the Male God. This is probably the most universal of all Wiccan symbols.

The Moon is considered to be the Mother of all life that exists on our earth. The Moon is closely tied to the Spiral of Life (birth, death, rebirth). The Moon is thought to both guide all our dreams and grant our wishes.

Night

A classic symbol in Wicca. Night is a time known for magick and mystery, when ordinary rules fail to apply. It is the realm of the Star Goddess. It's said that secret wisdom will shine from the moon and stars at night, making it a natural time for most Wiccans.

Numbers

All numbers can be considered sacred for one reason or another. Here are just a few numbers and what they symbolize.

Three – This number is considered important because the Goddess will manifest itself in three different aspects. Those three being The Maiden, The Mother, and The Crone.

Four – This is considered to be a number of completion. There are four elements, four directions, and four phases in life.

Five – This is a sacred number. The reason being it contains not only the whole earth (the number four), but also includes a fifth element. That element being the spirit.

Thirteen – A widely known Wiccan symbol. This number honors the Moon and how it cycles thirteen times during a year.

Owl

Known for their wisdom, Wiccans view them as a symbol because Owls can see what is hidden to those that have normal sight. Owls are considered to have the powers of an oracle, great wisdom, and a knack for averting evil. It is thought that Owls will share there visions with a Wiccan who honors them. This makes them popular as a Wiccans Familiar.

Pendulums

This is less a Wiccan symbol and more of a Wiccan tool. These are used by Wiccans for dowsing and when their trying to receive some guidance. Wiccans also use these to help sense auras. There's many different uses for Pendulums.

Psychic Powers

Many outsiders associate Psychic Powers with Wiccans. This is for good reason. Many Wiccans develop these skills naturally over time as they become more in harmony with the world around them. Wiccans practice being aware of the world around them, of being aware of their inner selves, and being aware of symbols that are sent from the Divine as a form of communication.

Raven

Another Wiccan symbol and a creature considered to be magickal. They are considered to be citizens of the world after ours. Ravens are said to travel between both the world of the dead and the living. This gives them great power and knowledge on transformation.

Runes

Also know as the Wiccan alphabet. It's used as a substitution cipher in order to help protect their magickal writings from anyone trying to pry. It's also known as the Theban alphabet. Runes play an important role in Wicca.

Salt

This is a Wicca symbol of the Mother's blood. Sharing salt is said to help create a lasting bond of kinship, as you're both sharing one Mother's blood. Salt is used as a purifying agent. It is thought to free items from decay and contamination. It is often used for blessing altars, bells, and a host of other things.

Seed

This is an important Wicca symbol that represents eternal life and reincarnation. As things like flowers die their seeds will live on and begin new life.

Spider

Another Wicca symbol. It is said that one could know the future if they knew how to read it in the spider's web. It's this magickal weaving and knowing of our world and its future that associates spiders with Wicca. Wiccans are also known to reweave the reality around them.

Star

These are pentagrams that are associated with Night, making them an ideal symbol for Wiccans. Stars are symbols of the potential every single being has to become Divine, with all the magickal power and wisdom that will entail.

Stone

These are often used as the Earth element on a Wicca altar. Since Stone is part of the Earth, they are seen as having healing properties.

Tarot Cards

Popular among Wiccans as a way to communicate with the Divine. This makes it an important Wiccan symbol. The philosophy contained in Tarot cards are very much the same to most Wiccan philosophies.

Tea Leaf Reading

Another form of divination, making it popular among Wiccans. It is closely associated with Witches making it an obvious Wiccan symbol.

Triple Goddess

The Maiden, The Mother, and The Crone. This is a major symbol in the Wiccan belief system. The Triple Goddess is often referred to as the Divine Feminine. She is shown in three different aspects, each representing different stages of life.

Triquetra

Is a Wicca symbol that generally makes reference to the Triple Goddess. It is also said to denote the three different levels of being. Those are mind, body, and spirit.

Web

Connected to Spider's the Web is another symbol of Wicca. The Web represents our world and all the different destinies being weaved. It is also used to symbolize our interdependence and interconnection. If you only destroy one web it has large scale effects collapsing much of the web around it.

Wiccans will often perform weaving spells in order to re-create their own lives. They do so to help heal the earth. This is a symbol that is very closely associated with the concept of the "Wheel of Life".

Witch's Hat

A typical Wiccan symbol. A Witch's Hat is pointy, almost created in the shape of a pyramid, which are known to help raise energy frequencies. The point of the hat is meant to funnel in the Divine energy. The Witch's hat is thought to increase one's intelligence.

Chapter Five: Wicca & Magick

In this chapter, you will learn:

- Wicca & Magick
- Types of Magick
- Casting A Circle
- Spelling Casting Preparation
- Crystals & Magick

Wicca & Magick

Wiccans believe that there's an essence running through everything, a power that's a piece of the Divine. This unites all things with each other, making everything and everyone connected on some level. Wiccans believe that by getting in touch with our gods or working magick, we can begin to tap into this essence ourselves.

Most Wiccans will describe every type of work we do with energy to be magick. This includes whether we're casting a circle, working on a practical spell, or performing a ritual. Others view magick to be only spell casting itself. Many Wiccans will practice some form of spell casting, however you aren't required to do so. How frequently or infrequently you cast spells is completely up to you or the coven you're a part of.

Now I know many of you think believing in magick is ridiculous, but in the context of what we're discussing as Wiccans, magick plays a large role in many of our daily lives. Now you won't be able to do the crazy things you see in movies, like shoot fireballs or turn someone into a tree. Instead, magick is something that comes with limitations on both its uses and effectiveness. Magick won't solve all your problems, and the results won't always be presented to you in an easy to see manner.

Magick requires concentration, dedication, and belief. If what you're doing means nothing to you then you won't accomplish anything. It's not simply saying a spell by repeating the words and actions that makes it effective, it's our will, and power of intention that helps to evoke the outcome we want.

Magick itself works better when used on yourself. It becomes less effective when cast on others. The time and effort that you spend on a spell will make you a lot more aware of any changes you'd like to see in yourself. Also, when it's a spell you've cast on yourself, you're much likelier to do all the non magickal things needed in order to attain the goal of your original spell. Magick is there to put you on the right path. It's not a free pass to get what you want without putting in the required time, work , and energy.

The relationship seen between miracles, prayer and magick can be complicated because they stem from the same well, but are approached using very divergent avenues. Magick is viewed as a command or an expression of our will, prayers are really just a request, and miracles are something we have no direct control over ourselves.

Types of Magick

In this section I'm going to briefly go over some of the many forms of magick one can practice. I'm sure this list is missing a few different kinds of magick, however, I wanted to give you a good idea of all the different forms out there and what they entail. Check out the resource section at the end of this book for some links to places you can find more information on this subject.

Animism

This is more belief system than way of working magick. However, it's a vital part to how many forms of magick work. It's the belief that all things whether inanimate or animate have a spiritual essence.

Astral Projection

This is a form of out of body existence where one assumes that there's an existence of another astral body that is separate from the physical form of our body, and is able to travel outside it. Wiccans practice this to by projecting their consciousness outwards.

The reason a Wiccan may engage in astral projection is in order to try and meet their Gods, learn more about life, learn more about nature, as a form of meditation, or as part of a ritual. There's a lot of different reasons, what you decide to use it for is up to you.

Augury

This is an old form of divination that studied the flight patterns of birds. What you would do is put out food for the birds and as they came to eat it you would ask yourself a "Yes" or "No" question.

After they all had finished eating and flew away, if they flew to the right your answer to the question was a "Yes" and if they flew to left then your answer to the question was a "No". If for some reason they scattered, you'd need to either rephrase the question and try again or there simply wasn't enough information for an answer.

Binding

This type of magick was used to cause someone from either causing harm to some one else or themselves. It can also be a positive act, in the case of binding together two different people.

A few popular forms of binding are:

Using a particular rune that is charged with keeping someone restrained.

Using a spell tablet that restricts someone from performing any type of harmful actions.

Using a candle that is inscribed with someone's name.

Black Magick

This is often described as magick that's done in a negative perceived manner.

Some forms of this magic can include:

Magick used to cause harm or destruction. These forms include cursing someone or hexing them.

Magick that invokes the spirit realm for negatives reasons.

Magick that is used to impact a person's free will.

Magick that eliminates or restricts the actions of the people around them.

Blood Magick

Many believe this type of magick holds a great amount of power as blood is often considered to be the essence of life in man. This type of magick is usually used by Wiccans trying to connect themselves completely to something else. It's often used for consecrating Wiccan tools and locking them to their owners. Blood magick is taboo in many circles as it's seen as having too much power.

Candle Magick

One of the simplest forms of spell casting. This type of magick is easier to perform than many other forms, not requiring a lot of tools or rituals. With candle magick you're deciding on a goal, declaring your intent, visualizing the end result, and focusing your intent or will in order to see the desired result achieved.

In candle magick different size candles and different color candles have different meanings or purposes.

Here is some color correspondence for candle magick:

Orange Candles – Encouragement and attraction.

Pink Candles – Sweet love and friendship.

White Candles – Truth and purity.

Green Candles – Abundance, financial gain, and fertility.

Gold Candles – Solar connections, business endeavors, and financial gain.

Yellow Candles – Protection and persuasion.

Silver Candles – Lunar connections, intuition, and reflection.

Darker Blue Candles – Vulnerability and depression.

Lighter Blue Candles – Patience, health, and understanding.

Red Candles - Courage, lust, sexual love, and health.

Black Candles – Banishment and negativity.

Purple Candles – Ambition and power.

Brown Candles – Animal or earth related magickal workings.

Cartomancy

This is a form of divination that uses a card deck. Each of the cards are assigned their own meanings. It is then up to the person reading the cards to interpret what the cards mean as they come out.

Here is an general example of how you can interpret what each card means in a normal deck of cards. I just want to note that some forms of Cartomancy involve different types of decks and some will reverse what the interpretations are on a regular deck. This brief guide is not a definitive one by any means.

Card Meanings:

Suit: Clubs

Ace – This indicates fame, wealth, and lots of friendships. It also indicates the feeling of being well known, and the ability to get perks because of your social status or looks.

King – Represents a close friend. This can be a long time companion, a trusted source who can be counted on when times get rough.

Queen – Represents a girlfriend of wife for men. For women it represents a sister or a close friend.

Jack – Represents a close friend. This is a person who excels at cheering you up.

10 – This represents good fortune and happiness. Also can be representative of a fun journey.

9 – Represents trouble or arguments with a close friend. It can also signify a lost relationship or unresolved disputes.

8 – Represents desperation. Can also represent an urgency for money.

7 - Represents good luck. Can also represent success if not ruined by someone of the opposite sex.

6- Represents partnership. This can signify success based on friendship and common goals.

5 – Represents marriage. Can also signify the start of a strong lasting alliance.

4 – Represents danger, failure, misfortune. Can also signify a friend turning there back on you or impeding your success.

3 - Represents a second or third marriage. Can also represent a new engagement.

2 - Represents bad luck. It can also signify opposition from your family and friends, or getting let down by someone close to you.

Suit: Spades

Ace – Represents the loss of a person close to you, an illness, or bad news.

King – Represents a man causing issues in your relationship or marriage.

Queen – Represents a women who interferes. For men, this could be a women who uses them to get something they want. For women, this can be a betrayal of someone they thought of as a close friend.

Jack – Represents someone who is getting in your way. Doesn't mean they are bad, instead it's someone hindering progress. It's someone that is lazy and does nothing but take without giving anything in return.

10 – This is an unlucky card. If this card falls near a card that is good it can cancel that card out. Near bad cards it can make things even worse.

9 – This is the worst card possible. It represents misery, loss of money, illness. Even when near the best cards this card means lack of success and defeat.

8 – Represents traitors, false friends, and someone willing to betray you. Trouble can be avoided if it's caught in the early stages. Examine all your close relationships thoroughly.

7- Represents quarrels and sorrow. Avoid any fights with your friends. If an argument arises let them think they've won for the time being.

6 – Represents a lot of planning with a lack of results. Signifies discouragement and hard work without success or profit.

5 - Represents love or success in one's business ventures. These things come after hard work and a lot of time invested.

4 – Represents a small misfortune. This can signify a setback that is temporary, or a brief illness.

3 – Represents unhappiness or misfortune in marriage or love. It can also signify a loss of hope or pride. It's time to move on and not dwell.

2 – Represents a total forced change. Can signify a change in relationship status, location, or death.

Suit: Diamonds

Ace – Represents an important message. This can mean the arrival of a gift, package, or letter. The contents of this message are extremely important.

King – Represents a fierce rival and competitor. For a woman, this can also mean a lying lover or abusive man.

Queen – Represents a flirty woman, someone that can interfere with your plans. This can also signify someone who likes to gossip and is attractive to men. These people are able to pull the wool over a man's eyes and get away with interfering.

Jack – Represents a bearer of bad news. Can also signify someone selfish. This person can be a problem to woman but is harmless to men.

10 – Represents money. Can signify greed or money being the main force of a particular partnership.

9 – Represents adventure. Can also signify a move with the hope of future advancement.

8 – Represents traveling and a later in life marriage. Can signify needing to get away and settle down but being to busy to do so currently.

7 – Represents bad luck in regards to an idea or undertaking. Can also signify a unreliable man who drinks or gambles.

6 – Represents an unhappy early in life marriage that won't last long term. Can also signify a second unhappy marriage.

5- Represents long lasting friendship and prosperity. Can signify success with raising children or a pride in one's family.

4 – Represents fighting or feuds. Can signify neglected or forgotten family and friends. Tensions bubbling under the surface may be brought to a boil.

3 - Represents a card of quarrels and disputes. This can signify legal actions or lawsuits. It can also be a sign of divorce or separation.

2 – Represents a major love affair that either leads to interfering in another marriage or ending in marriage itself.

Suit: Hearts

Ace – Represents a person's environment or home. Can signify an address change or a visit.

King – Represents someone with influence and power that can do a good thing for a woman.

Queen – Represents a woman who can be trusted. Can signify someone faithful and knowledgeable. This represents a woman who believes in playing fair.

Jack – This represents a good friend. This can be a confidant or someone close, either family or friend. This is someone they've known since their youth.

10 – Represents good luck. This is a good card and can counteract some of the bad cards that are around it.

9 – Represents harmony. This is called a wish card. When surrounded by other bad cards, it can represent obstacles you'll need to deal with if you want your wish to get fulfilled.

8 – Represents a celebration or an event. Signifies something that's already being planned or is being worked on.

7 – Represents disappointment. Signifies a person or partner failing to live up to their prior promises. If you're dealing with a plan you can expect the other person you're relying on to back out.

6 – Represents a warning. Can signify someone trying to take advantage of you. Can also mean you're being overly generous without getting something back for it. You're essentially be used.

5 – Represents indecisiveness. Signifies someone unable to make up their mind on something. Can also represent someone who's about to break plans you've made with them.

4 – Represents an old maid or bachelor. This can signify someone who is being overly picky when choosing a partner. This person may be destined to be alone.

3 – Represents unwise decisions. These decisions are made quickly and without having the proper information needed on hand.

2 - Represents success that is somehow beyond what you were expecting. If it's surrounded by bad cards it may delay you reaching your goals.

Contagious Magick

This type of magick involves objects that come into contact with a person and can still influence them afterwards. This type of magick is performed by absorbing energy out of objects like an amulet, crystal, or talisman. It can also be used to call forth the power of an animal, like a lion, to give a person strength and courage, or like a bird, to help set a person free from something holding them down.

Defense Magick

This is magick used to defend one self. Some forms of defense magick include shielding, blocking and warding. Some items of defense include iron, salt, silver, light, fire, a pentacle, crystals, and gemstones.

Shielding – Creates a energy shield around someone to block any types of energy that causes them issues.

Blocking – Similar to shielding, only more physical in nature. With blocking you physically put yourself in-between you and what is causing you distress. This gives you both benefits of energy shielding with an obstruction that is physical thrown in for more blocking power.

Warding - Forming an energy bubble to divert energy, causing it to veer from you direction. For example casting a circle is a form of warding.

Dowsing

Dowsing is not strictly for finding water like many people think. Many Wiccans practice dowsing with pendulums, rods, and even their fingers. It's been shown that dowsing can help to also find minerals, and can use our extrasensory perception skills to make other discoveries.

Dowsing involves using a series of "Yes" and "No' questions. Your dowsing tool will then respond to your questions with movement. Depending on what the movement is you'll know the answer. For example, if your dowsing rods cross each or swing outwards then the answer happens to be a "Yes". However, if the dowsing rods don't make any movements then your answer is "No". By doing this over and over you'll eventually find what you're seeking out.

Elemental Magick

This is a popular and natural form of magick, harnessing the power of one of the four elements. This magick is simpler to perform than many spells that use herbs, stones, or oils. However, these spells can still be quite powerful.

Fire

Fire magick is used for spells that involve energy, creativity, passion, strength, and anger. Other items besides candles that are used for this form of magick include volcanic glass and an Athame.

Air

Air magick is used used for creativity, inspiration, ideas, travel, intelligence, new beginnings, clarity of the mind, and freedom. Items used include incense, bells, quartz and feathers.

Water

Water magick is used for friendship, love, healing, fertility, and sleep. Some of the items used include certain crystals, lilac, a chalice, and natural rainwater.

Earth

Earth magick is used for responsibility, money, nature, rules, prosperity, and growth. Some of the items used include stones, a pentacle, a bowl of rock salt or earth, herbs, and certain crystals.

Geomancy

This is a form of divination where you interpret the markings found on the ground around you, or what types of patterns form after tossing handfuls of rocks, soil, and sand.

Healing Magick

This is magick used with the intention of healing either your mind, body or soul. Some types of healing spells include spells to stop drinking or smoking cigarettes. I'll go over a great resource for finding spells you can use in the resource section at the end of this book.

Herbalism

Herbs are often used in practicing magick for there essences and vibrations. Herbs, like animals, have a gender, an element, are ruled by a particular planet, and are oftentimes sacred to a Goddess or God. In Wicca this is known as herbal correspondence, and it plays a crucial role in most Wiccan spells. Nurturing and growing herbs in your personal magickal garden is also seen as giving you an advantage of having personal energy influencing whatever plants you're growing. For example, a plant like Angelica, that is ruled by our Sun, will then have all the influences of fire and the Sun, along with your own personal energy.

Ways Wiccans Use Herbs

Sachets and Charms – Fill up a small bag, using the correct material or color, with the herbs to make either a sachet or charm. Then you can carry your charm on you, keep it hung in the house, burn it or bury it. What you do with it all depends on spell your are performing and the purpose of the spell.

Bath – Make your sachet, then place it in your healing or ritual bath. Use certain herbs for certain purposes. Fragrant herbs such as lavender will make a relaxing bath. Using eucalyptus in your bath is good when you have the flu or a cold.

Oils – Place your herbs in a oil, then let them sit for a few days before straining. You can then use this to make beauty oils for your body, anointing oils for any ritual work, or flavor oils for seasoning and cooking.

Incense – You can burn herbs as ritual incense. One example is sage smudge, which can be used to help clear out any negative vibrations occupying a certain space.

Teas – You can use different herbs to make effective teas for healing sicknesses. Some teas can also be made to help you alter your state of consciousness.

Smoking – You can make herbs into smoking mixtures that can also help alter your state of consciousness.

Common Herbs Used By Wiccans

Angelica Root – Masculine / Fire / Sun

Used in exorcism and protection incense. Can also carry as a talisman of protection. You can smoke this herb's leaves to have visions. You can also add it to a bath in order to remove a hex. Don't use this herb in large doses. It has some health side effects, especially in pregnant women.

Basil - Masculine / Fire / Mars

This herb is used in prosperity and love spells. You can carry this to help attract wealth. People also sprinkle this over there partners to keep them faithful. This herb is popular for purification ritual baths. It's thought to either bring about new love or to help set you free of a love you no longer want.

Bay Leaves – Masculine / Fire / Sun

This herb is used in potions made for wisdom, clairvoyance, and visions. Many place it under their pillows in order to have dreams of what's to come. You can also carry this herb to ward off any evil. This herb is also good in cleansing baths and teas.

Blessed Thistle – Masculine / Fire / Mars

Used in hex breaking, purification, and protection. This herb works well in healing spells. It's great for fighting gallstones, nausea, and migraines

Burdock – Feminine / Water / Venus

This herb is good for healing and protection. Works especially well on any foot ailments you may be suffering from.

Bramble – Feminine / Water / Venus

This is a powerful protection herb. Can also be used to help attract and gain more wealth.

Camellia - Feminine / Water / Moon

Used to help attract prosperity and money. Is also good for treating certain skin conditions.

Caraway – Masculine / Air/ Mercury

Used for protection against harmful spirits. You can use these seeds for ensuring a partner's faithfulness. Is popular in cooking for inducing lust.

Catnip – Feminine / Water / Venus

This herb is used in animal magick. Good for healing your pets and increasing your bonds psychically with your pets. Can also be used in different teas for relaxation and happiness. Popular herb for creating love wishes.

Cedar – Masculine / Fire / Sun

Used for attracting money, love, protection, and purification. Is known for curing nightmares when burned as incense.

Chamomile - Masculine / Water / Sun

Extremely popular in teas. Known for its relaxing properties. Is also used to attract wealth and grant prosperity wishes. Also useful for breaking hexes or curses that have been cast on you.

Cinnamon – Masculine / Fire / Sun

Used for healing, success, lust, power, love, and protection. Is also known as a popular male aphrodisiac.

Cloves – Masculine / Fire / Jupiter

Used for love, protection, good luck, and money. Can be worn to help repel any negative energy that's around you. Can also be worn to attract someone of the opposite sex.

Comfrey Leaf – Feminine / Air / Saturn

Strong protection herb against negativity of any kind. Also good for healing strains, sprains, sores and fractures. I also like to use it in teas for an upset stomach.

Cumin – Masculine / Fire / Mars

Often burned for protection. Is popular in love spells to help induce lust in others. Can also mix with some salt in order to keep away bad luck and evil spirits.

Dandelion Leaf – Masculine / Air / Jupiter

Used for calling spirits, wishes, and divination. This can also be used to help increase psychic abilities. Also a good herb for healing and sleep.

Dill – Masculine / Fire / Mercury

Often hung in doorways to help protect a home. Can also be carried on your person for protection. Popular herb in lust and love spells. Is sometimes used to attract money.

Dried Fig – Masculine / Fire / Jupiter

Used in love and fertility spells. Great for divination and a popular herb used in certain spell bags.

Eucalyptus Leaf – Feminine / Moon / Air

Used to fight infections, kill germs, and ease congestion in the lungs. Is a great herb for protection. Can also be used for cleansing and purifying any space of negative energy.

Fennel Seed – Masculine / Fire / Mercury

Used for longevity, vitality, courage, strength and virility. Is often used to help prevent possession, curses and ward off negativity. Can also be used to deal with weight loss, bad breath, and digestion issues.

Feverfew – Feminine / Water / Venus

Used for protection and love. This is also a good herb for both spiritual healing and regular healing. This can ward off many illnesses and help strengthen the immune system.

Flax Seed – Masculine / Fire / Mercury

Used for absorbing negative energy. Good for protection and healing spells. Also a good herb for your health and lowering cholesterol.

Garlic – Masculine / Fire / Mars

Used for protection and healing. Often associated with warding off vampires.

Ginger – Masculine / Fire / Mars

Used for success, love, power, and money. Often eaten before spell casting to increase the power of a spell.

Ginseng – Masculine / Fire / Sun

Used for longevity, potency, and rejuvenation. People will carry this herb to enhance beauty. Also burned to ward off bad spirits and break curses. Good for digestion and treating depression.

Holly Leaf – Masculine / Fire / Mars

Used in dream magick and for luck. Also is great as a protection herb. Used to keep away poison, lightning, and evil spirits. Not a herb for consumption.

Hops – Masculine / Air / Mars

Used for healing and spells. Good herb for sleep issues.

Horehound – Masculine / Earth / Mercury

Used to increase strength and energy. This herb is good for increasing focus and concentration. Also used to help treat colds, asthma, sore throats, coughs, and bronchitis.

Juniper Berries – Masculine / Fire / Sun

Used in protection magick. Also good for easing arthritis, intestinal cramps, and digestion.

Mandrake Root – Masculine / Fire / Mercury

Used for love, protection, health and fertility. This herb is used to intensify the magick of spells. When carried will help attract courage and love. Also hung in the home for prosperity and protection.

Mullein – Feminine / Fire / Saturn

Used for courage and protection. Used to ward off nightmares and demons. Also used in divination and healing spells. Good for stopping diarrhea, soothing hemorrhoids, and healing lungs.

Nettles – Masculine / Fire / Mars

Used for purification and to remove curses. This is good for skin issues, anemia, and allergies.

Nutmeg – Masculine / Fire / Jupiter

Used for health, money, and luck. Used to help strengthen psychic powers. Can be used as a hallucinogen in teas. This is toxic in big doses. Only use a pinch.

Orris Root – Feminine / Water / Venus

Used for divination, protection and love. Can be added to a bath in order to increase your personal protection.

Passion Flower – Feminine / Water / Venus

Used for promoting peace, emotional balance and prosperity. Used in many love spells. Also good for relieving hysteria, nerve pain, and aiding with sleep issues.

Peppermint – Masculine / Fire / Mercury

Used for love, purification, psychic power, and sleep issues. This herb is also very helpful for heartburn, an upset stomach, congestion, and nausea.

Pine – Masculine/ Air / Sun

Used for fertility, prosperity, and healing. This can be burned for reversing negative energy and gaining more strength.

Raspberry Leaf - Feminine / Water / Venus

Used for promoting sleep, protection, love, and healing. Also used in childbirth. Good for dealing with nausea, diarrhea, and vomiting.

Rose Petals – Feminine / Water / Venus

Used for protection, luck, love, and healing. Popular in love magick and for clearing dizziness, headaches, and mouth sores.

Rosemary – Masculine / Fire / Sun

Used for lust, purification, sleep, healing and protection. Good for cleansing and purifying. Often used to heal halitosis, headaches, and aid in depression.

Sage – Masculine / Air / Jupiter

Used for wisdom, longevity, prosperity, and protection. Often used in money and healing spells. Good for healing wounds, easing joint pain, easing muscle pain, and reducing fevers.

Scotch Broom Leaf – Masculine / Air / Mars

Used for protection and purification spells. Also burned to calm down the wind. Can be used in teas for inducing psychic powers. Only use this herb in moderation, otherwise it can become toxic.

Seaweed – Feminine / Water / Moon

Used for protection on the water. Used to summon sea winds and sea spirits. Also popular in money spells. Good for relieving rheumatism.

Spanish Moss – Masculine / Earth / Jupiter

Used for banishing spirits, money, and luck. Many find this to be a great herb for bringing luck with gambling.

St. John's Wort – Masculine / Fire / Sun

Used for protection, health, love, strength, and divination. Used in teas to help treat sickness and depression. Can be burned to help banish negative energy and negative thoughts.

Star Anise – Masculine / Air / Jupiter

Used for purification, luck, protection, and psychic powers. Also used as a diuretic and stimulant. Helps relieve flatulence and promote digestion.

Tea – Masculine / Fire / Sun

Used for strength and courage. Good for scrying. Used in teas for it's antioxidant compounds.

Thistle Flower – Masculine / Fire / Mars

Used for defense and protection. Is also used for financial and spiritual blessings. Is often burned to counteract any hexes.

Thyme – Feminine / Water / Venus

Used for healing and purification. Also can be worn to help increase a person's psychic abilities.

Valerian Root – Feminine / Water / Venus

Used for sleep protection and dream magick. Often used for purifying a ritual space. Is a popular tranquilizer and muscle relaxant.

Vanilla – Feminine / Water / Venus

Used for seduction, love and mental powers. Often worn as an aphrodisiac and fragrant oil.

White Willow Bark – Feminine / Water / Moon

Used for protection, divination, love, and healing. Is often used in spells for attracting love. Can be burned with sandalwood to help conjure up spirits. Helps to ease joint pain, arthritis, and muscle pain.

Yarrow Flower – Feminine / Water / Venus

Used for negative energy, sorrow, and depression. Can be worn to repel negative energy. Is used to help stop baldness and cure colds.

Illusionary Magick

This involves glamouring parts of the physical world using your will and intent. Some Wiccans don't put much stock in this form of magick and believe it to be closer to movie and performer magic.

Kitchen Magick

Growing in popularity. When you use your own natural ingredients, you have the opportunity to infuse the dishes with your will and intent. Many people will make a kitchen alter and use measures to make the kitchen space sacred.

Knot / Cord Magick

This is a common form of folk magic associated with the weather and wind. These spells are prepared in advance, then used whenever needed. You untie each knot releasing the entrapped power held in the cord during the course of nine straight days.

For cord magick you'll want a cord to normally be 9 feet long, and the color that is right for whatever magick you're trying to accomplish. You should be the only one to use your cord. Always consecrate your cord to your specific purpose.

Lithomancy

This is a form of divination in which stones are cast to clearly see your past, understand the present, and predict your future.

Music Magick

Music is considered very magickal. Songs and chants can bind your intention to different vibrations. Popular among many Wiccans.

Naming

Names contain power. To know more about yourself is incredibly powerful. Taking a name intentionally is like working a spell. Every time you say the name it reminds you of who you've chosen to be. The energy from this helps the universe make you into the person you want to be. Choosing a name aligns you more with your true divine essence.

Necromancy

This is the magickal practical of trying to communicate with the dead. Often used as a form of divination. Is closely aligned to black magick and voodoo. The word necromancy literally means corpse divination.

Number Magick

Also known to many as numerology. Is a form of divination that uses numbers. Every number from 1 up to 9 has it's own energy and meaning. This can be used to help determine your path in life.

Palmistry

Another form of divination. Used for reading palms. Good form of divination for beginners. Is easy to learn and even newbies can get pretty accurate readings with only a small amount of practice.

Pendulum Magick

A form of divination using pendulums. Uses "Yes" or "No" questions to divine answers to your questions. You can make your pendulum yourself or purchase one inexpensively.

Rune Magick

Can be used for divination or as a part of charms. This is an ancient form of magick. You can draw the runes, or use rune stones, or rune cards. This can be a difficult form of magik to master.

Some Common Runes Symbols and Their Meanings:

Algiz – Symbol - Z

Used for protection, victory, good luck, personal strength, and success

Ansuz – Symbol - A

Used for clarity, wisdom, communications, and increasing magickal energy.

Berkana – Symbol - B

Used for fertility, abundance, protection, and growth.

Daeg – Symbol - D

Used for prosperity, expansion, growth, and turning in a new direction.

Ehwaz – Symbol - E

Used for abrupt changes, moving, and travel.

Eihwaz – Symbol – I

Used for foresight, banishing magick, and removal of delays and objects.

Fehu – Symbol – F

Used for possessions and wealth. Also used for sending energy.

Gebo – Symbol – G

Used for partnerships, gifts, sex magick, and balance.

Hagall – Symbol – H

Used for avoiding disruptions, and asking for fate to lend a hand with an issue out of your control.

Kenaz - Symbol - K

Used for healing, artistic pursuits, passion, strength, and creativity.

Ing – Symbol - NG

Used for fertility. Also used as a positive ending to a situation or issue and the beginning of a new one.

Isa – Symbol - I

Used for cooling relationships, division, separation, and cessation of energy.

Jera – Symbol - J & Y

Used for abundance, fertility, and the culmination of an event.

Lagaz – Symbol – L
Used for creativity, intuition, passion, and imagination.

Mannaz – Symbol – M

Used for teamwork, cooperation, new projects, and collaboration.

Neid – Symbol – N

Used for fulfilling needs, sex magick, and motivation.

Othel – Symbol – O

Used for protection of possessions and inheritance.

Perdhro – Symbol - P

Used for hidden secrets being revealed, unexpected gains, and spiritual evolution.

Raido – Symbol - R

Used for movement, safe travel, and obtaining justice.

Sigel – Symbol – S & Z

Used for power, victory, health, strength, vitality, and production.

Thurisaz – Symbol – Th

Used for luck, protection, and opening gateways.

Tir – Symbol – T

Used for leadership, increased finances, passion, and success.

Uruz - Symbol - U or V

Used for strength, creating change, magickal energy boost, vitality, and healing.

Wunjo – Symbol - W or V

Used for happiness, joy, love and fulfillment in home and career.

Sympathetic Magic

For this magick you draw a picture of what you want, then visualize receiving it with as much will and intensity as you can muster. Often used for money, business, property, love, and health. Is not meant to be used to affect someone's free will.

Weather Magick

Can be used for forecasting and divination. Also used to try and actually control the weather.

Casting A Circle

Wicca is an ever expanding religion as it allows its practitioners to experiment and add new lore and knowledge to that of its ancestors. However, when it comes to some of the basics like casting a circle there's no reason for reinvention. One of the main Wicca techniques used is casting a circle before any energy workings, divination sessions, or spell castings.

Casting a circle is important because it helps to keep evil spirits and negative energy at bay. If you have good intentions and you come at nature with respect and love, there's no way for evil spirits to gain access to your circle. Casting a circle is also important because it gives you a space that you won't get disturbed by any of your personal thoughts. It's a space where you gain focus and concentrate on achieving whatever it is you've set out to do. Basically casting a circle will let you get results faster and more safely.

Steps for casting a circle:

There are several ways to do this. I'll just give you one here as an example. Feel free to use whatever methods work best for you.

Locate the four different quarters - South, North, East, West. Use a compass if you need help with this step.

Starting with the North, turn in each direction, bow and say something to the effect of "I cast this circle in the names of both light and love, may it help protect and guide me from any unwanted spirits." Feel free to put it into your own words, just keep the general meaning intact.

Once you've done this once in each of the four different directions, face to the North., point with your wand, scepter, or hand at the earth, imagine yourself as the center point of your circle and turn clockwise three times.

While you're doing this feel the energy as it rises from the line you've just cast. It's now safe to begin performing any of your Wicca rituals, spells, or ceremonies.

Once you're finished, you'll need to open your circle again. Keeping a circle closed means that you're wasting both the Earth's and your own energy. When opening a circle, face north, thank all the spirits for their assistance, then turn counter clockwise three times with your hand, scepter, or wand pointing towards the imaginary line.

Casting a circle is an extremely important part of Wicca. It's recommended you do so every time you work with an energy or spell. Many Wiccans will also cast a circle for dowsing and divination. You always want to keep yourself safe. So it's always best to cast a circle.

You can make your circle as big as you need it to be. For larger circles, mark your center point with an object and proceed to walk the circle yourself three times around clockwise.

When part of a Wicca coven and the casting involves multiple Wiccans you can either let your priest or priestess be the one to cast the circle or you can join hands with your fellow practitioners, while one member remains in the center, the others move so they form a clock hand.

Spell Casting Preparations

In this section I'm going to go over how to get properly prepared to cast a spell. I'll discuss what you need to do, when you should do it, and what items you should use in order to cast a spell. Different things like money and love require you to do separate things, at separate times, with different type of items. Again, this isn't guide on how to cast a particular spell just some of the things you want to do in advance to get prepared. Every spell is different and has it's own specific things that need to be done in order for it to be successful. Check out the resources section for where to find the spells you want to use and what you'll need to do to use them.

When preparing to cast a spell, the very first thing you need is intention. You need to know what you want and have a detailed image of it in your mind. You need to be able to trust your intuition. It's crucial you believe completely in what you're trying to do and the magickal powers you're planning on working with.

Keep a positive state of mind, and hold faith in yourself. If you need something to help get you in the proper mindset, calming oils can create a relaxing setting. I prefer rose, jasmine, or lavender. Pick whichever you prefer.

The next thing you need is an area to practice your magick. This can either be an outdoor area or place in your home. Make sure there's enough room for your altar. These can be as simple or elaborate as you'd like. Ours started off rather simple and became more elaborate over the years. An altar is normally placed facing the Northern direction.

On your alter place two candles, one at each end of your altar. Keep them in a reliable candle holder. Then you need to get four different colored candles. Each of these candles will represent one of the four elements.

Red Candle – South – Representing Fire

Green Candle – North – Representing Earth

Yellow Candle – East – Representing Air

Blue Candle – West – Representing Water

I also like to have a female and male statue on different ends of my altar to help represent the deities I'm calling upon, and as representation of the yin and the yang energies being used. Another symbol you'll want to include is a pentacle. This is a powerful Earth symbol and can be either worn or placed on the altar.

Now before you get ready to begin casting your spell, imagine a circle of white light that is surrounding you and acting as a form of protection. This will allow you to focus more and increase energy. You may also want to burn incense, as it helps create a more beneficial atmosphere for spell casting.

Don't forget to cast a circle before working on your spell. See the above section on casting a circle for more information on that process. Once that's complete it's time to beginning casting your spell.

Each type of spell has it's own requirements and things that should be done in order for it to be successful. There's no one size fits all. Check out the resource section for some great spell casting resources you can use to guide yourself further in the process.

Crystals and Magick

Crystals are an important tool that most Wiccans use. They are used in energy work and during your spell casting to add some extra potency to what you're casting. Crystal generate amazing energy and can enhance any spell.

Remember when selecting your crystal, let the crystal choose you. You'll find that you're drawn to certain crystals and there energies. Don't fight this, instead go with your intuition.

A few different crystals and there purposes.

Agate – Used for balancing emotions and protecting your mind. Good for expelling and repelling negative thoughts.

Amber – Used for protection and healing.

Aventurine - Used for fostering balance and caution. Good for money management.

Black Kyanite – Used for protection and changing negative energy into positive energy.

Black Obsidian – Used for protection spells and repelling restless spirits.

Bornite – Used for absorbing negative energy. Good for using when nervous or unsettled.

Chrysoprase – Used for attracting money. Also used for relieving stress and calming nerves. Good for fostering energy and new partnerships.

Citrine – Used for attracting wealth and handling finances.

Hematite – Used mainly in love spells. Helpful for improving relationships.

Jade – Used for marriage and the union of two people.

Larimar – Used for drawing your soul mate closer and spiritual love.

Moonstone – Used for enhancing sexuality and igniting passion.

Rhodochrosite – Used for opening the heart to a new love and aligning oneself emotionally, physically, and mentally.

Rose Quartz – Used for inducing love and other love spells.

Scolecites – Used for enhancing the energy between two different people and for healing.

Smoke Quartz – Used to manifest dreams and desires. Also used for removing and blocking negative energy related to finances. Helpful with new partnerships and new ventures.

Tiger's Eye – Used for fostering patience and prosperity.

Chapter Six: Wicca Study Cheat Sheet

In this chapter, you will learn:

- Wicca Study Cheat Sheet

Wicca Study Cheat Sheet

Learning and growing is a never ending process. There's always some way to improve and and become better in your craft. This section will give you a quick cheat sheet on what things you need to study and learn in order to become a Wiccan. Remember becoming a Wiccan is a long process. Many people take years of study before being accepted into a coven. Once you become a Wiccan the learning process doesn't end. There's always new spells, rituals and techniques you can learn.

Many people don't know where to begin or feel overwhelmed by the sheer amount of information on the subject. This cheat sheet is designed to simply let you know what areas you should start learning more about. There are many good Wicca schools and online courses available if you want to go that route. I'll be sure to mention a few in the resources section.

Background Information

In order to become Wiccan one must understand its traditions, beliefs, history, and rituals. Some areas of study you focus your studies on should include:

Wiccan terminology.

Wiccan traditions, mythology, and ancient cultures.

Different forms of Wicca and their belief systems.

Common misconceptions – reality vs. myth.

How Wicca works in modern times.

What it means to be Wicca / What it doesn't mean.

The Belief Systems

What are a Wiccans core beliefs. What makes their religion different from other religions. Here are a few of the topics you should begin educating yourself on.

Wicca vs. other religions.

Wicca & spirituality.

Deities – The God & Goddess – Building a relationship with them.

The role of reincarnation in Wicca.

The Three Fold Law / The Wiccan Rede / The Law of Return.

Magick & Symbols – There place in Wicca.

Herbs / Stones / Crystal / Oils – There purpose and uses.

The Elements / Role of nature in Wicca.

Wicca Tools

There are many tools used in Wicca. Some are for casting spells, other are for rituals. Knowing what each tool is, there purpose, how they should be used, and when they should be used is extremely important.

Ritual Tools – When / Why / How.

Consecrating / Charging / Cleansing items.

The role of Magick in Wicca.

Proper Wicca clothing

Types of Magick and their differences.

What is a Book of Shadows?

Magickal correspondences.

Sacred Space

Having the proper area to work in is incredibly important as a Wiccan. Here I'll give you a few topics you need to know about to further your education.

Casting circles.

Ritual spaces.

Special rooms.

Basic Altar layout.

Prepping & Cleansing.

How to properly cast a spell.

Different casting methods.

Different purposes.

Different energy centers.

Holidays

A big part of Wicca is understanding their holidays and the importance those days hold. Here I'll give you a few topics you need to know about if you want to become a Wiccan.

The Wiccan Calendar

Sabbats & Esbats – When they are / Why there important.

Types of Rituals.

Holidays in relation to other religions.

Rites of Passage

Coven vs. Solitaire vs Groups

How you practice your craft is ultimately up to you. However, you should know the in's and out's of practicing both with a coven and on your own. Here's some things you should begin researching before making any final decisions.

What does each one entail.

Pro's and cons – Groups / Covens / Solitaire

How to practice as a Solitaire

How to figure out what groups and covens are good and which are wrong for you.

What degree systems do they use and how do they differ.

Rules, ethics and proper etiquette.

Where to find a study group

Online communities vs local communities.

How and when to let other people know your beliefs.

Finding a proper mentor – Where to look and what to look for.

Finding classes, workshops, and online courses.

Divination

Not all Wiccans choose to do this but it's an important part of the culture and something that needs to be learned by anyone trying to become a Wiccan.

Forms of divination (scrying, tarot, astrology, runes, palmistry, etc.)

Channeling – What it is and how it works.

Interpretations – Proper methods.

The importance of dreams.

Psychic abilities.

Exercises to increase and improve abilities.

The importance of symbols – Meanings and Uses.

Magick & Spell Casting

Here's a list of areas you'll need to start studying. Magick plays a big part of most Wiccans lives. This is an area of research that will be ongoing, as the amount of information is almost endless.

Intent – Focus & Will.

Types of Energy Work.

Types of Magick.

Banishing & Cleansing.

Healing & Herbalism.

Enchanted Objects – Talismans, amulets, etc.

Familiars.

Finding your Wiccan name.

Personal power.

Different types of magick (elemental, lunar, solar, ceremonial, candle, etc.)

Releasing energy

Invocations.

Hexes & Curses.

Centering & Grounding.

Witches' Pyramid.

Correspondences

Moon Phase Correspondences.

Candle Correspondences.

Planetary Correspondences.

Daily Correspondences.

Elemental Correspondences.

Crystal Correspondences.

Herbal Correspondences.

Essential Oil Correspondences.

Incense Correspondences.

Food Correspondences.

Animal Correspondences.

Number Correspondences.

Metal Correspondences.

Tree Correspondences.

Tool Correspondences.

Mineral Correspondences.

Color Correspondences.

Chapter Seven: Wicca Resources

In this chapter, you will learn:

- Wicca Resources

Wicca Resources

In this section I'm going to list a bunch of resources I've found over the years that added value to my education and path towards becoming a Wiccan. I'm sure there's many other options that won't be mentioned. Feel free to use as many or as few of these as you want. Some of these are completely free resources, while others are books you'll need to purchase, courses you'll need to pay for, or items you might want to have. I don't have affiliation or make anything off the sites and books I've listed below. I've listed these here because either myself or my friends have used or read them over the years and found them to be beneficial.

All of these are easy to find by just searching the names I've listed in bold.

Websites

Spells of Magic – One of my personal favorites. Offers a ton of free resources you'll definitely want to check out. Everything from articles and videos, to online forums, an online shop, and an incredible free master list of spells with all the instructions and ingredients needed to cast them.

The Witches Voice – Excellent resource for networking with other Wiccans.

Covenant of the Goddess – One of the oldest organizations for Wiccans around. This is a legally recognized national org1anization of Wiccan churches, Wiccan covens, solitaries, local councils and clergy in many cities that are able to provide some basic general information and resources.

Llewellyn – Company that offers a ton of excellent books and products for sale related to Wicca. I've purchased a variety of things off this site over the years and have been always been pleased.

13 Moons – Online Wicca marketplace. My personal favorite.

Wiccan Place – Online Wicca marketplace to pick up any supplies you might need.

Online Classes / Courses

Luna's Grimoire Free School of Magick and Witchcraft– Great free introduction course to Wicca. Offers a lot of valuable information.

The College of Sacred Mists - Online Wiccan college offering a variety of courses to someone wanting to further there education at home online.

Our Lady Of Enchantment – Online Wiccan Seminary offering classes in a variety of courses.

Books You Should Read

The Woman's Encyclopedia of Myths and Secrets by Barbara Walker

The Woman's Dictionary of Symbols and Sacred Objects by Barbara Walker

These are two of the most definitive resources available regarding symbolism from a Wiccan perspective. You'll have a difficult time thinking of a Wiccan symbol that isn't covered in these two books, although I'm sure there are a at least a few. Two books that should be in any Wiccans reference library.

Encyclopedia of Magical Herbs by Scott Cunningham

The Master Book of Herbalism by Paul Beyerl

The Healing Power of Herbs by Michael T. Murray

Three excellent resources on herbs and herbalism. These books taught me a ton and are frequently referenced throughout the year while preparing my rituals and spells.

Drawing Down The Moon by Margot Adler

Wicca: A Guide for The Solitary Practitioner by Scott Cunningham

Buckland's Complete Book of Witchcraft by Raymond Buckland

The Triumph Of The Moon by Ronald Hutton

Conclusion:

You've reached the end! Thanks again for purchasing my book. Hopefully you've gotten a good crash course into what Wicca is and what Wicca isn't. While becoming a Wiccan isn't for everyone, for those that practice the craft it's a transformative experience.

Hopefully you'll be able to take some of the information from these pages and run with it. Remember, become a Wiccan is a lengthy process filled with studying and hard work. It isn't for everyone. However, if you think it's for you, I wish you nothing but the best.

I hope I was able to help you in your journey!

Printed in Poland
by Amazon Fulfillment
Poland Sp. z o.o., Wrocław